ELVIS

NEWLY DISCOVERED DRAWINGS OF ELVIS PRESLEY

BY BETTY HARPER

BANTAM BOOKS • NEW YORK • LONDON • TORONTO

ELVIS: NEWLY DISCOVERED DRAWINGS OF ELVIS PRESLEY

BY BETTY HARPER

ELVIS: Newly Discovered Drawings of Elvis Presley
A Bantam Book/December 1979

Introduction by Len Leone

ISBN 0-553-01241-X

Published simultaneously in the United States and Canada

Bantam Books are published by Bantam Books, Inc. Its trademark, consisting of the words "Bantam Books" and the portrayal of a bantam, is Registered in U.S. Patent and Trademark Office and in other countries. Marca Registrada, Bantam Books, Inc., 666 Fifth Avenue, New York, New York 10019.

PRINTED IN THE UNITED STATES OF AMERICA

For Elvis—

—A vital inspiration

in the development of my talent!

Barry

I would like to express my sincere appreciation to the following people for their friendship and assistance in this collection.

Marilou Anastario • Linda Harper • Bob Hendricks •
Carolyn Johnson • Klyde Koone • Jody Miller •
Ken Owen • Jim Ritz • Harold Williams •

To Brian, my husband and friend, for his love, understanding and belief in who I am,

To my parents who encouraged my art through its years of growth and...

Especially to my children, Brian Jr., Esther, Bridget and Loretta Lynn...For I want them to realize that within these pages is not only a man who created a generation but my life as well — to know and understand my work they will know and understand me.

Betty Harper

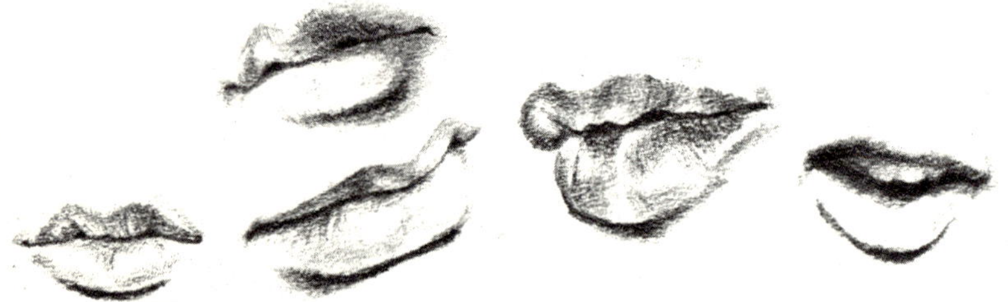

Unless you have been vacationing on Mars for the last two decades, you will know that there has been an incredible amount of material written about Elvis Presley. A lot of it was written before August 16, 1977, and much more since that date. This is not an attempt to rehash facts most of us are familiar with, or embellish anecdotes that subsidize legend. The "Loving Accounts" have been mostly too loving and the "Sensationalized Accounts" have been mostly too sensational. Yet somewhere in the middle lies the blatant fact that everyone seems to have missed: Elvis Presley was a simple man!

Everybody is concerned with trying to find out what made him tick, or what were the psychological overtones to his existence. Some studies even take a metaphysical approach.

Yet nowhere in this plethora of literature (and I have read most of it) does anyone deal with a singularly important and intriguing area: What did Elvis Presley think of himself? How did he feel about the contributions he made to that auspicious group we know as the human race?

Recently, I was involved with a motion picture project that brought me into contact with many of the people with whom Elvis Presley had surrounded himself. Most of them, like the man himself, are good people. A few of them are outstanding human beings. We would talk at great length about Elvis, and I would enjoy the pleasant memories and the funny stories they would relate to me. Then I would ask them the aforementioned questions and a sudden silence would come over them. It was a hard topic for them to get into, which leads me to believe that they, like his adoring public, really didn't know Elvis at all. I was never fortunate enough to have met Elvis, so I surely didn't presume I knew the answer, but I did know that if I ever heard the correct response a light would go off in my head, and I would say, "That's it!" But whatever the answer was, I knew it had to be simple. I had to stop looking at the forest and zero in on the trees.

The light in my head began to flicker when I received a registered package at my office at Dick Clark Productions. It contained some drawings and a letter introducing me to the artist, Betty Harper. I read the letter and then looked at the drawings. I was astonished. I had seen many pictures and paintings of Elvis — some of them damn good — but these...well, these were Elvis Presley.

I was going to Nashville to record the music for the movie I was working on, so I called Betty. I felt I had to meet any person who could capture another person on a blank piece of paper with such detail.

Betty came to the recording studio. It had been a long, back-breaking day. She brought some more of her work — not copies as I had received in the mail but originals — and I was overwhelmed. It was an incredible sight to see the musicians and technicians (most of whom had worked with Elvis) and Felton Jarvis (who was Elvis's record producer, and my co-producer for this project) examining Betty's work. It was hard to get everyone back into the studio to finish the recordings. But once we did, we did the best tracks of that long day. This little girl had provided the potion we needed to pound the adrenaline through our weary systems.

After we finished, I began to talk to Betty. She and I were sort of in the same boat. We had been great admirers of Elvis for most of our lives, but we had never met him. And it seemed strange to us that a man whom we only knew from an image flickering on a movie or television screen, and whose voice only communicated to us within the grooves of a black vinyl record, should have such a profound influence on our lives.

And then it happened. The light in my head blazed to its full candlepower. Betty said, "Well, that's what I think Elvis was all about. He was an inspiration to so many people." I knew she was right. I thought about my own life. I looked up to Elvis. I wanted to be like him. I wanted to do the things he did. When I was younger I thought that I wanted to do the superficial things that he did in his movies. When I matured, I realized that I really wanted to do the things he did artistically. Betty said the same thing. I looked at her paintings and knew what she meant. Elvis Presley's greatest gift was not his incomparable musical ability, his magnetic personal appearance, or his astounding good looks, it was his ability to inspire people to try a little harder, to be themselves and to do the best they possibly could. That's all Elvis did. He never tried to be anything he wasn't, and in finding himself he achieved what most men only dream of. It was so simple, it was beautiful.

Several months later I was talking to Priscilla Presley. Priscilla and I had become friends only recently, and I guess it never occurred to her that I had not known Elvis. I made her aware of the fact that one of my greatest regrets was not having met him. I told her I would just like to have been able to tell him what a positive effect he had on my life. She smiled and said, "He would have appreciated that. He was really so simple...so uncomplicated. He felt the most important thing he could do was to inspire people. He didn't mean it in a conceited way...in fact he felt it was more of an obligation than anything."

Isn't it wonderful to be right? I thought. But I have to give credit where credit is due — Betty Harper was the one who was right.

After I had gotten to know Felton Jarvis, he said to me, "If Elvis had known you, he would have liked you." I don't know if that's true or not, but I was very flattered. Although I never worked with Elvis himself, I feel that having come in close contact with so many of his associates affords me the opportunity to say I knew him a little. I know the kind of people he liked. He liked sincere people...he liked creative people...he liked inspired people.

Elvis would have liked Betty Harper.

James Ritz

James Ritz is a writer/producer who recently served as associate producer for the Dick Clark Production **"Elvis"** starring Kurt Russell. Along with Felton Jarvis, he co-produced the music for that film and the soundtrack album.

ARTIST AND MODEL (13'' X 15¾'')

When I first flew to Tennessee to meet with Betty Harper and to see and evaluate her work I walked through the door of her charming house and was immediately struck by the silent simplicity of her drawings. They were everywhere. Every imaginable space was occupied. Every. And the subject was always the same. Row upon row of Elvis peering down from the walls. Every possible mood was reflected. Every conceivable gesture was recorded. It was strange. Strange, because I felt for the first time I truly had now some new and very real understanding of this man. His power and personality were everywhere...his every nuance registered. All very precisely drawn and recorded by an artistic master of recollections.

Here was Elvis Presley. He had been captured and frozen in time, forever, by the simple medium of a...pencil in the small, delicate hand of a pretty, young lady from Tennessee. I couldn't believe it. I was awestruck... speechless. But I had to see them again. So I moved towards the first wall of drawings and this time I viewed them slowly...very slowly...yes, I was right the first time. This was a veritable feast for the eyes. They were indeed magnificent drawings. Magnificent. I was especially amazed at the juxtaposition of negative space. This critical and exacting display of composition is found all too infrequently in the young artist of today. For this quality of sophistication one must glance back to Ingres and Degas.

The artist's selectivity of what to leave in the drawings must be very sensitively realized. She had accomplished that.

I was singularly impressed with the quality of her perception. Her decisions were always sure. She seemed bent on always dealing with a vision that insisted on "delighting the eye." I found myself wanting to see more and more…and once again…more.

Flying back to New York later that day I couldn't help but think and wonder about these two…Betty Harper is an accomplished artist thanks to the impetus created by Elvis Presley… and Elvis Presley owes something to the art and energy of Betty Harper—immortality.

Len Leone

Len Leone is an artist/photographer/designer and art director. His drawings and paintings are in many private collections as well as in the permanent archives of the Salmagundi Club of Fine Art in New York City. His work has been on exhibition at The Society of Illustrators, The Hecksher Museum in Huntington, L.I. and the Salmagundi Club. He is currently art director and vice president of Bantam Books.

ABOUT THE ARTIST

Betty Harper was an Army brat. As she moved from place to place with her soldier father, she was formally trained in the great art centers of Europe. After graduating from Dreux American High School in Paris, she went to Abilene Christian University in Texas, where she met her husband Brian. Today they live with their four children in Hendersonville, Tennessee.

Known internationally for her celebrity portraits — especially of the Nashville music stars — Betty Harper has drawn more than 10,000 portraits of Elvis's "perfect face." "I want people to look at him and feel like he is going to smile or wink at them."

Every drawing she creates has its own special identity, a vivid, realistic rendering of human feeling which is distinctly "Harper."

IF I CAN DREAM (10½'' X 13½'')

SOFTLY (12⅛'' X 16¾'')

ACHIEVEMENT (10'' X 13'')

RESTRAINED (9¾'' X 12¾'')

Betty Porter ©

GETTING AWAY FROM IT ALL (9'' X 10¼'')

CONTEMPLATING (7-3/4 x 8)

WHO! ME! (10'' X 15'')

FREEDOM TO BE MYSELF (12" X 15")

Betty Harper ©

YOU DON'T KNOW ME (9½'' X 13'')

FLIRTATION (6″ X 10¼″)

DON'T BE CRUEL (7½'' X 9¾'')

THE GOOD TIMES (14'' X 19'')

THE STING (8⅛'' X 10¼'')

THE STUDY (6″ X 14⅛″)

WHEN WILL YOU SMILE AGAIN? (8″ X 14¾″)

THE GUITAR MAN (15'' X 20'')

PENETRALIA (6¾'' X 10'')

TO SEE YOU IS TO LOVE YOU (7″ X 16″)

SATISFACTION (8'' X 11'')
From the collection of James Ritz

Betty Harper ©

I BELIEVE IN YOU (6″ X 8″)

REFLECTIONS (10½'' X 15'')

TAKING CARE OF BUSINESS (20″ x 30″)

INTENSITY (10'' x 16¾'')

COME BACK TO ME (10″ X 10½″)

THE ENTERTAINER (10¾″ X 15″)

AFTER THE PERFORMANCE (5¼'' X 6¼'')

MOODY BLUES (8¼″ x 17½″)

SOLITAIRE (10½'' x 16'')

LOVE ME (4 11/16'' X 9'')

THAT CERTAIN SMILE (15" X 20")

Betty HARPER ©

WELCOME TO MY WORLD (20″ x 30″)

LONG LONELY HIGHWAY (12″ X 13½″)

LEGENDARY PERFORMER #1 (30″ x 40″)

MR. SHOWMAN (8½′′ X 9⅛′′)

I BELIEVE (11 ¼'' X 15'')

PERFORMER AND LOVER (12″ X 19¼″)

WHERE COULD I GO BUT TO THE LORD (15″ x 19″)